OBJECT LES
VERY YOUNG CHILDREN

OBJECT LESSONS FOR VERY YOUNG CHILDREN

SHERYL BRUINSMA

BAKER BOOK HOUSE
Grand Rapids, Michigan 49516

Copyright © 1988 by Baker Books
a division of Baker Book House Company
P.O. Box 6287, Grand Rapids, MI 49516-6287

ISBN: 0-8010-0956-1

Eighth printing, August 1994

Printed in the United States of America

Scripture verses in this volume are based on the
King James Version of the Bible

Contents

Using Object Lessons to Teach

Using objects to hold children's attention is an effective way to teach children spiritual truths. Like the biblical parables, using familiar objects and drawing spiritual parallels makes it easier for children to understand abstract concepts.

The lessons in this book are designed for very young children—simple, direct, and uncomplicated. As an aid in presentation, each lesson contains an outline which will help begin a presentation, remember the basic parallel, and end on an effective note. Each lesson concludes with a challenge which may be used to extend the lesson. Having to *do* something with the concept presented will aid the child in understanding and remembering what has been taught. A complete and specific section on how to give children's object lessons has been included in my first book *New Object Lessons for Children of All Ages*, published by Baker Book House in 1980.

Many of the lessons under Special Days could effectively be presented anytime of year without reference to the special day. For example, the lesson on patience for advent could be given as a lesson on patience alone at any time. Concepts such as prayer, thanksgiving, the love of God, the power of the Holy Spirit, and so forth, are always relevant.

Teaching the
Three-to-Five-Year-Old Child

Teaching very young children presents a unique challenge. In order to have an impact on their young minds, it is important to internalize the needs of these learners. The following tips are presented to aid in making your presentations effective.

Choose *one topic* and stay with it. One idea well taught stands a much better chance of being comprehended and remembered.

Keep the *message simple*. Young children are able to relate only to simple concepts. If you get too complicated, they will just focus on something else. Pare away unnecessary information that might confuse them.

Use *uncomplicated objects*. The purpose of the object is to get their attention and to make a direct comparison so that they will remember the lesson. If young children get overinvolved with the object, they become distracted from the lesson.

Make sure your *vocabulary* is on their level. If you use words they do not understand, they will not know what you are talking about.

Keep the *lesson short*. Children at this age have a short attention span. You will lose them if you talk too long. You may still need to call back their attention with phrases such as: "Look at this!" "Did you hear me?" "Would you like that?"

Keep your *words relevant* to the object and the lesson. Children are distracted by their own thoughts. An unrelated comment could sidetrack them from what you want to say. Avoid asides or using the children to entertain the adults.

Continually *repeat, restate,* and *review* the concept. Young children learn and remember from repeated exposure.

Use material that is suitable to the needs and interests of *your children*. Get to know them, and they will help you develop the lesson material. There is a wide range of interests and ability between young children.

Be *enthusiastic* and excited about what you have to say. Convey the feeling that what you are teaching is important. Young children learn a great deal from your tone of voice and your gestures.

Enjoy the lessons in this book. They have been presented to give you ideas and to demonstrate appropriate presentations at this challenging level. God loves the little children, and so will you!

The Lord's Prayer

Many children grow up hearing the Lord's Prayer repeated. Before it becomes a meaningless ritual for them, it is important to teach them to think about and relate to these words.

Often children begin to memorize the Lord's Prayer as they hear it. It is a good idea, however, to reinforce learning the correct words with additional repetition either before or after the presentations or by Sunday-school teachers or parents.

Even for children who are unfamiliar with the Lord's Prayer, it holds many important concepts that can be understood by young children.

1

The Lord's Prayer

Our Father Who Art in Heaven

Object: a man's hat (or an article of clothing, and so forth, which represents a kind father to your children)

Lesson: God the Father

Outline

Introduce object: This is a father's hat. It belongs to the father of a very large family.

1. A father loves and cares for his children.

2. God is a heavenly father—even more powerfully loving and caring.

3. *Conclusion:* Think of the best father or daddy you know of, and then think of one even *better* and *more powerful.* Then you will know why we say, "Our Father, who art in heaven."

This is a father's hat. It belongs to a father of a very large family. I brought it with me today to help you understand what is meant by the first line of the Lord's Prayer which is "Our Father, who art in heaven."

A good father is someone who loves his children and

takes good care of them. He talks to them, teaches them what to do, gives them the things they need, punishes them when they do wrong, so that they will learn, and tells them the right things to do. Doesn't that sound like what a good father does? When I was your age I called my father "Daddy." Do you call your father "Daddy"?

God is our heavenly Father—a very special Daddy. Even though he has many children, he loves *each* one of us. He is a father who knows and cares about what each of his children is thinking and doing. He gives us what we need and listens to us when we have a problem. He tells us what to do and then expects us to do it. He loves us and wants us to love him back. He cares for you and you and you [*point to each child or call them by name if possible*].

Think of the best father, or daddy, you know of and then think of one even *better* and *more powerful*. Then you will know why we say, "Our Father, who art in heaven."

Challenge: Let's pray together now, calling God our "heavenly Father."

2

The Lord's Prayer

Hallowed Be Thy Name

Object: a picture of Princess Diana of England (or the president of the USA or other well-known person. *Your tone of voice is very important to this concept.*)

Lesson: *Hallowed* means reverence, awe, love.

Outline

Introduce object: Do you know who is in this picture?

1. If Princess Diana were in this room you would be excited and say, "Wow, this is wonderful!"

2. "Hallowed be thy name" means excitement, reverence, awe, and love of God *(shown in tone of voice).*

3. *Conclusion:* Hallowed be thy name is a way of saying "God, you are a wonderful father. We love you. We are excited that you are here with us."

Do you know who is in this picture? It's Princess Diana of England. Wouldn't it be exciting if she walked into this room? Just think of how excited you would feel! Imagine seeing a *real* princess. I wonder what she would be wearing. I wonder if she would speak to us.

The feeling of "Wow, look at that—a real princess" is what we mean by "Hallowed be thy name" [*tone of voice demonstrates reverence and awe*]. "Hallowed be thy name" means we feel all tingly and excited just thinking about how wonderful God is. It means that we love God so much that his name is very special to us. It means that we hope everyone is as excited about our God and wants to love him as we do.

"Hallowed be thy name" is a way of saying, "God, you are a wonderful Father. We love you. We are excited that you are here with us."

Challenge: Practice saying "hallowed be thy name" with love and excitement in your voice. Have your family say it too.

3
The Lord's Prayer

Thy Kingdom Come.
Thy Will Be Done on Earth As It Is in Heaven

Object: the game of "Simon Says" *(This game is based on a series of simple directions. When preceded by the words* "Simon says," *the directions are followed. A child is out of the game if he/she fails to complete a direction preceded by "Simon says" or if the directions are followed when "Simon says" was not said first.)*

Lesson: Do God's will.

Outline

Introduce object: How many of you know how to play "Simon Says"?

1. In the game everyone wants to do what "Simon Says."

2. In this part of the Lord's Prayer we want everyone to do what God says.

3. *Conclusion:* It's too bad that not everybody does what God says. I hope you can do it.

How many of you know how to play "Simon Says"? [*Explain the game if they do not know.*] Now let's try it. Simon says *stand up*. That's right, you all stood up. Simon says *jump up and down*. Good, you're all still in the game. Now, *sit down*. Whoops! I didn't say *Simon says* first, so those of you who sat down are out of the game. In this game you must do whatever Simon says and only if *Simon says* comes first.

The part of the Lord's Prayer in which we say, "Thy kingdom come, thy will be done on earth as it is in heaven," means that we would like everyone to do what God wants just like in the game everyone has to do what Simon says. Think of how wonderful the world would be if everyone did what God wants just as they do in heaven. God says *no fighting*. God says *no unkindness*. God says *love everybody*. God says *feed the hungry and help the poor*.

Let's invent a new game called "God Says." God says *smile at the person next to you*. God says *give somebody a hug*. *Hit somebody*. No, God didn't say that so I'm glad you didn't do it!

Sometimes someone doesn't do what Simon says and gets out of the game. It's too bad that not everybody does what God says. I hope you can do it.

Challenge: When you go home, play the new game of "God Says."

4

The Lord's Prayer

Give Us This Day Our Daily Bread

Object: a loaf of bread *(pita bread or unsliced bread might make the object more interesting)*

Lesson: God provides for our needs

Outline

Introduce object: Is anybody hungry? I have a loaf of bread with me.

1. Since bread is something we need every day, we pray for it.
2. When we ask for bread, we mean whatever we need for healthy bodies.
3. *Conclusion:* We ask God for what we need and we know he will give it to us. Isn't that great!

Is anybody hungry? I have a loaf of bread with me. With this loaf of bread I can make lots of good things to eat like a peanut butter sandwich or a bologna and cheese sandwich. I can make toast and put jelly on it. I could also have just a piece of bread with butter. Yum!

We eat bread every day. It is an important part of our

food. That's why the Lord's Prayer says, "Give us this day our daily bread." We are asking God to give us the bread we need each day so we won't be hungry.

Would you like to eat bread and only bread every day? I hope not. We need other food too. We need milk, meat, fruit, vegetables, and so forth. When we say, "Give us this day our daily bread," we don't mean only bread. We are asking for whatever we need to have healthy bodies so we can grow and be strong. We don't need to make a list of all the foods for God. He knows what we need to be healthy—yes, even those vegetables that we don't always like to eat!

We ask God for what we need and we know he will give it to us. Isn't that great!

Challenge: Have a "thank-you sandwich." The next time you have a sandwich, say "thank you" to God for the bread and whatever is in between it.

5

The Lord's Prayer

Forgive Us Our Debts, As We Forgive Our Debtors

Object: a magic slate *(a child's toy with which you write on the top, pull up the sheet, and the writing "disappears." If one is not available, a small chalkboard and eraser could be substituted.)*

Lesson: Forgiveness

(Note: The word *trespasses* is actually more meaningful because it denotes walking on an individual's rights as a person. However, the wording should be in keeping with what the children hear.)

Outline

Introduce object: A magic slate can be fun. You write on it, pull up the top sheet, and what you have written disappears.

1. God forgives our sins and they are gone—just like the writing on the magic slate.

2. You must also forgive others in this way.

3. *Conclusion:* It's not easy to forgive in the same way that you want God to forgive you.

A magic slate can be fun. You write on it, pull up the top sheet, and what you have written disappears. It is gone completely. You can't see any of it.

In the Lord's Prayer when we say, "Forgive us our debts, as we forgive our debtors," we are asking God to forgive us for the things we do that are wrong. That's what "debts" means.

When we do something unkind or don't do what our parents want, we say we are sorry. Then we ask God to forgive us. And do you know what he does? He forgives us! He forgives us and makes what we have done go away, just like what I have drawn on this magic slate.

There is more to this part of the Lord's Prayer. "Forgive us our debts *as we forgive our debtors*." That means that we have to forgive other people—just as we want God to forgive us. If someone takes a toy of yours, you need to forgive them—even if they break it! Could you forgive them and then not think about it anymore? That's not an easy thing to do. It's not easy to forgive in the same way that you want God to forgive you.

Challenge: Remember to do this: The next time someone says they are sorry, say back to them, "I forgive you." [*This can be acted out.*]

6

The Lord's Prayer

And Lead Us Not into Temptation, But Deliver Us from Evil

Object: suntan lotion *(or mosquito repellent)*

Lesson: God protects us.

Outline

Introduce object: Because I burn very easily, I have to wear suntan lotion whenever I go out into the sun for very long.

1. Suntan lotion protects you from sunburn.
2. We ask God to protect us so we won't get "burned" by harmful people, places, or things.
3. *Conclusion:* When we ask God to protect us and we *know* he will do it, we *will* be kept safe from harm.

Because I burn very easily, I have to wear suntan lotion whenever I go out into the sun for very long. Does your mother put suntan lotion on you when you go to the beach? The lotion protects your skin from getting burned by the sun. A bad sunburn can make you very sick. It hurts too!

In this part of the Lord's Prayer we ask God to "Lead us not into temptation, but deliver us from evil." *Temptation* means something that we might want to do or have, but it would be wrong. *Evil* mean something bad. We want God to protect us from bad people and places and things so we will not get "burned" or hurt. We ask God to help us choose the right friends and to be in places where nothing bad will happen to us. Then when you are in a place and something inside of you says it is wrong—we know God is telling you to get out of there fast!

When we ask God to protect us and we *know* he will do it, we *will* be kept safe from harm.

Challenge: Take some "pretend" lotion. As you pretend to rub it in say to yourself, "God will protect me." Of course, it is God's love for you and your prayers to him that will protect you—not the "pretend" lotion!

7

The Lord's Prayer

For Thine Is the Kingdom, and the Power, and the Glory, for Ever.

Object: a hymnal

Lesson: We praise God because he wants us to, and it makes us happy.

Outline

Introduce object: You can't read this yet, but when you can, a hymnal will become a very important book.

1. We praise God when we sing and pray to him.
2. Praising God makes us happy. God wants us to praise him.
3. *Conclusion:* It is wonderful to sing and to pray and to praise God!

You can't read this yet, but when you can, a hymnal will become a very important book. Do you know what this book is about? It has songs, some of them written a very long time ago because people have loved God for a very long time. These songs talk about God and how wonderful he is. They tell God we love him. They talk about how to

24

live a Christian life. When we say how great God is, that is called *praising him*. We do it by singing and praying and saying good things about him.

In the Lord's Prayer when we say, "For thine is the kingdom, and the power, and the glory, for ever," we are praising God. We are saying how wonderful he is, that he can do anything, and that we want everyone to know and to love him.

We praise God when we sing songs about him. We praise God when we say things like this about him. God *wants* us to do this. It shows him that we love him. It also makes *us* happy to do this. It makes us feel good to say how much we love God. It is wonderful to sing and to pray and to praise God!

Challenge: Have someone show you the song "Jesus Loves Me" in a hymn book.

8

The Lord's Prayer

Amen

Object: using a doll or a stuffed animal, nod the head

Lesson: *Amen* means approval.

Outline

Introduce object: I brought my little friend Teddy with me today.

1. Just as Teddy nods his head, the word *amen* means "yes."

2. *Amen* is also a time to pause and say that it is right.

3. *Conclusion: Amen* is a great word to use.

I brought my little friend Teddy with me today. Teddy can't talk but he does have something to say to you. Teddy, do you like these boys and girls? [*He nods his head.*] What does that mean? That's right, it means *yes*. What's that, Teddy? Boys and girls, he wants to know if you like him too. You are nodding your heads. That means, "Yes, I do." Would you like to play with Teddy? Those of you who nodded your heads are saying, "Yes, I would." You said a lot with the nod of your head.

The word *amen* comes at the end of the Lord's Prayer. It means what you meant when you nodded your head. It means: Yes, that's right. Yes, I mean this. Yes, everything I just said is true.

Sometimes we think *amen* means it's over, this is the end, we can eat now, it's time to go. It means much more than that. It is a time to stop and think about what you said—that it is finished and it is right. It is a way to agree with what has been said. *Amen* is a great word to use.

Challenge: The next time you hear the word *amen*, say it along and know what you mean by it—that you are saying *it is right*.

The Ten Commandments

The word *commandments* is usually not in the vocabulary of young children. They often have occasion to hear the word, however. Take the time to teach it to them. Tell them that it means "things God wants you to do." Have them repeat the word until they can say it correctly. Children enjoy learning new words when they have a use for them.

The following lessons are presented as a series. They can also be given as individual lessons whenever you have a need for them.

9

The First Commandment

Commandment: You shall have no gods except me.

Object: something your children would want (toy, candy, money)

Lesson: God wants to be *first* in your life.

Outline

Introduce object: I have a remote control car with me today. If you could Have anything you wanted, what would it be?

1. God wants to be most important in your life.

2. When you think of God first, you are a more kind and loving person.

3. *Conclusion:* God wants you to love him most. Then you will be happy and *things* will not be important to you.

I have a remote control car with me today. If you could have anything you wanted, what would it be? I really like this car. It's not mine but if I did have my own, I could have a lot of fun with it. It's all right to have toys—just as long as they are not the most important thing in your life. God wants to be that.

We will be talking about the Ten Co
Commandments are things that God wants
you say the word *commandments*? First, God
most important in your life—more impo
anything else you have or want, like a new bike
animal or a special doll.

Now, God knows what he is talking about! If Go
important in your life, you will think first of him a   what
he wants you to do. That will make you a kind and loving
person—the kind of person God wants you to be.

If you have too many things, you will have to spend too
much of your time and energy taking care of them, keeping people from taking them, and thinking about how to
get more. God wants you to love him most. Then you will
be happy and *things* will not be important to you.

Challenge: Let's make up a cheer for you to say on your way
back home: God is Number One! God is Number One! God
is Number One!

10

The Second Commandment

Commandment: You shall not make yourself a carved image or any likeness of anything in heaven or on earth beneath or in the waters under the earth; you shall not bow down to them or serve them. For I, Yahweh your God, am a jealous God and I punish the father's fault in the sons, the grandsons, and the great-grandsons of those who hate me; but I show kindness to thousands of those who love me and keep my commandments.

Object: Soak an egg in vinegar for a day or until the shell becomes soft enough to gently rub the calcium off and the egg becomes transparent

Lesson: God knows what is in our hearts.

Outline

Introduce object: Have you ever looked inside of an egg that is *not* broken?

1. God can see into your heart like we can see into the egg.
2. God wants to find in your heart that you love him and want to keep his commandments.
3. *Conclusion:* Will God be happy with what he finds inside of you?

Have you ever looked inside of an egg that is *not* broken? You can't do it unless you have a specially prepared egg like this one. I had to soak the egg in vinegar for a long time and then carefully rub off the softened shell. Now it feels like rubber and will break very easily—but you can see into it.

The second commandment, or what God wants us to do, has lots of words. What it means is that God can see into your heart. What he wants to find there is that you love him and want to keep his commandments. Just as you can see what is in the egg, God can see what is in your heart. God wants you in your heart to love and praise and worship and follow him. Will God be happy with what he finds inside of you?

Challenge: The next time you have an egg, think of the yellow part as a big ball of love for God which he can see in *your* heart. [*Draw an egg.*]

11

The Third Commandment

Commandment: You shall not utter the name of Yahweh your God to misuse it, for Yahweh will not leave unpunished the man who utters his name to misuse it.

Object: a bar of soap

Lesson: Do not misuse God's name.

Outline

Introduce object: What could I do with this bar of soap?

1. God wants you to have a clean mouth.
2. God wants you to use his name only when you are talking to or about him.
3. *Conclusion:* It's a good thing that you won't need a bar of soap to keep your mouth clean!

What could I do with this bar of soap? I could wash my hands before I eat. I could use it in the shower or in the bathtub. I remember how my mother used a bar of soap one time. I said a bad word, and she used soap to wash out my dirty mouth. It tasted terrible. Did any of you ever taste soap? Well, let me tell you—I never said that again. I never

34

forgot about keeping my mouth clean by not saying bad words.

In the third commandment God tells us not to use his name in a wrong way. Whenever we use God's name it should be to talk to him, to talk about him, or to praise him. You should never use God's name because you are angry or upset or surprised or to prove that you mean what you say. God does not want you to do that. Your parents do not want you to do that. Your teachers do not want you to do that.

You wouldn't want someone to use your name when they got upset like: For Mike's sake, don't do that! Jane, I'm so angry! I swear to Sue, it's true. John James, that hurts! [*Use the children's names.*] That sounds silly, doesn't it! But people do that to God.

Do you do this? I'm glad you don't. It's a good thing that you won't need a bar of soap to keep your mouth clean!

Challenge: When you wash yourself with soap, say, "Clean hands, clean mouth."

12

The Fourth Commandment

Commandment: Remember the sabbath day and keep it holy. For six days you shall labour and do all your work, but the seventh day is a sabbath for Yahweh your God. You shall do no work that day, neither you nor your son nor your daughter nor your servants, men or women, nor your animals nor the stranger who lives with you. For in six days Yahweh made the heavens and the earth and the sea and all that these hold, but on the seventh day he rested; that is why Yahweh has blessed the sabbath day and made it sacred.

Object: bunch of grapes

Lesson: Sunday is God's day.

Outline

Introduce object: I have a hand full of seedless grapes. There are so many that when I take one out you won't even miss it.

1. God only asks for one out of seven.
2. God wants this so we will have a special time to remember him and to rest.

36

3. *Conclusion:* Think of it this way. The word *sun* is part
   of Sunday. It is a sunny day because it is God's day.

I have a hand full of grapes. There are so many that
when I take one out you won't even miss it. I still have a
bunch left.

The fourth commandment says that God wants one day
out of seven. One grape out of seven is hardly missed. One
day out of seven is not much to ask.

Why does God want us to do that? He knows that we
need to rest at least one day out of seven. We would get
very tired and not be able to do well on our jobs. In fact,
you will go to school five days a week—that gives you two
days off!

More important, God wants us to spend this day thinking about him, remembering him, going to church, and
singing songs about him. That makes Sunday a very happy
day. Think of it this way. The word *sun* is part of Sunday. It
is a sunny day because it is God's day.

Challenge: Let's play a game. Count to seven. Each time you
get to seven, stand up and clap because it is God's day. [*Dis-
tribute grapes.*]

13
The Fifth Commandment

Commandment: Honor your father and your mother so that you may have a long life in the land that Yahweh your God has given you.

Object: Give a child something fragile to hold or something to carry that might spill

Lesson: Honor your parents.

Outline

Introduce object: Who will hold this vase for me?

1. Taking care of this vase is a big job, but your parents have an even bigger job.

2. God wants you to honor them—to make them happy.

3. *Conclusion:* Your parents do their best for you. You should do your best for them.

Who will hold this vase for me? Thank you for your help. Now, I have to tell you that this vase cost a lot of money. It is very old, and that makes it worth more money. It was my mother's vase, and I would be very upset to lose it. How does that make you feel about taking care of that vase? Let me remind you that if you drop the vase it will break into hundreds of little pieces. Yes, if you had to hold this vase for a long time, it would be a big job.

God has given your parents an even bigger job. God has given them *you* to hold, to take care of. This job will last at least eighteen years. That is why the fifth commandment tells you to honor them. That means to love them, to do what they say, and to try to make them happy. This will make their job a little easier and help them live longer.

Your parents do their best for you. You should do your best for them.

Challenge: Go and give your parents a big hug.

14

The Sixth Commandment

Commandment: You shall not kill.

Object: a small kitten or puppy

Lesson: God wants you to be gentle and kind.

Outline

Introduce object: Look at this cute little kitten.

1. The kitten makes us feel gentle and kind. This is how God wants us to feel.

2. God wants us to feel kindness for all, even those who are not nice to us.

3. *Conclusion:* It is not easy to feel and act kindly toward bullies and mean people but that is the best way to act. God knows what he is talking about!

Look at this cute little kitten. It is so sweet and helpless. You can't help but say, "Ahhh." This cuddly little ball of fur with the soft, round eyes makes you want to be kind and gentle. It makes you feel soft and warm inside. It makes you want to take care of it and protect it. This is the kind of feeling God wants you to have.

The sixth commandment says, "You shall not kill." You

might think, "That's no problem. I'm not ever going to kill anybody." I certainly hope you won't, but the commandment means more than that. God wants you to have a kind and gentle spirit for everybody, even for people who are not nice to you. It's easy to feel kind towards soft, little kittens and cheerful, nice people. It's not easy to feel and act kindly toward bullies and mean people but that is the best way to act. God knows what he is talking about!

Challenge: Feel this soft little kitten and look into her big trusting eyes. Remember this gentle feeling.

15

The Seventh Commandment

Commandment: You shall not commit adultery.

Object: a wedding ring

Lesson: Marriage is an important commitment *(promise)*.

Outline

Introduce object: The object I want to show you is on my hand. It is a wedding ring.

1. God wants us to take marriage seriously.

2. When you get married you promise to love *that* person and want the best for them.

3. *Conclusion:* Marriage is serious and important. You must think hard and really mean it, when you promise to love and care for someone all your life.

The object I want to show you is on my hand. It is a wedding ring. Do you know why I wear one? It stands for a promise I made to my husband and to God on the day that I was married. Wearing this ring reminds me of it every day.

Marriage is one of life's biggest events. In the old days the church bell rang for the three biggest events in life—

being born, getting married, and dying. There is not much you can choose about your birth or death, but you must choose carefully whom you will marry. It is an important and lasting promise. Choose someone you will love forever.

The sixth commandment tells us to do this. It tells us to take our wedding seriously. When you get married before God, you promise to love only that person, to care for that person, and to think about the needs of that person. You need to work hard at having a happy marriage.

Challenge: Look carefully at a wedding ring and see that it has no ending. Remember that a wedding means you will love that person with no ending.

16

The Eighth Commandment

Commandment: You shall not steal.

Object: a collection plate with money in it

Lesson: Do not steal.

Outline

Introduce object: Here is today's collection plate with all of the money people put in it.

1. Taking money from the plate would be stealing.

2. God wants you *never* to take anything that does not belong to you.

3. *Conclusion:* God wants you to be honest and not take or keep something that belongs to someone else.

Here is today's collection plate with all of the money people put in it. What would you think if I kept some of the money? Yes, that would be stealing. It would be a terrible thing to do.

I'm glad you know that it would be wrong to take this money. It doesn't belong to me. It belongs to the church. In the eighth commandment God says, "You shall not steal." You may not take anything that is not yours.

Sometimes you find something. Does that mean you can keep it; or should you try to find out who lost it? If your puppy ran away and somebody found him, should he keep him? If you drop your new pencil when you get up and leave the room, should I keep it? If I find a toy under the table, what should I do with it? Yes, give it back. Look for the owner. Don't keep it. God wants you to be honest and not take or keep something that belongs to someone else.

Challenge: (Drop money on the floor.) What will you do with this money?

17

The Ninth Commandment

Commandment: You shall not bear false witness against your neighbor.

Object: Pick a child and tell a false story about what he/she did.

Lesson: Tell the truth.

Outline

Introduce object: Boy, do I have something to tell you about [Pat!]

1. It is wrong to tell lies about people.

2. It is wrong to tell part truths or give false impressions about people.

3. *Conclusion:* My father always said, "If you don't have anything good to say about a person, don't say anything at all."

Boy, do I have something to tell you about [Pat!] Yesterday I saw him in the park, and do you know what he was doing? He was eating worms!

Did you do that, [Pat?] Of course not. How did it make you feel when I told everyone you did? It was not a nice feeling, and I was very wrong to do that. I'm sorry. I just did that to tell you about the ninth commandment. In the ninth commandment God says not to tell stories about your neighbors. It can get *them* in trouble and *you* in trouble—everyone gets hurt.

It is also wrong if the story is only partly true. In fact, it is still wrong to tell stories about people that are true, if it might hurt the person. If [Pat] really did eat worms, you might not want to play with him anymore. You might think he always ate worms. His feelings would be hurt if he didn't have friends.

My father always said, "If you don't have anything good to say about a person, don't say anything at all."

Challenge: Promise God that you will think twice before you say something about a person. If it's not true, don't say it. If it is true, make sure it is a good thing to say.

18
The Tenth Commandment

Commandment: You shall not covet your neighbor's house. You shall not covet your neighbor's wife, or his servant, man or woman, or his ox, or his donkey, or anything that is his.

Object: Choose a piece of jewelry, clothing, or toy that a child has and covet it (*overemphasize the word* want).

Lesson: Do not want something that belongs to another.

Outline

Introduce object: Julie, you have a beautiful necklace on today. I like it. In fact, I *want* it!

1. It is not right for you to *have* to have something that belongs to someone else.

2. When you think too much about things, like toys or jewelry or clothes, you forget about God.

3. *Conclusion:* God wants you to be happy with what you have and not waste your time wanting things.

Julie, you have a beautiful necklace on today. I like it. In fact, I *want* it [*tone of voice is important*]. I just *have* to have that necklace. I'm going to find some way to get it.

48

This is what is meant in the tenth commandment where God tells us not to want something that belongs to someone else. That doesn't mean that it is wrong for me to go and buy another necklace like Julie's, unless finding one becomes all that I can think about. It means that I can't keep wanting Julie's necklace. It belongs to her, and I have no right to it. If I want it badly enough, I might try to trick her out of it or to steal it.

The reason that God tells us not to do this is because it makes us mean and selfish people. We will soon do anything to get what we want. We begin to think *only* of what we want and forget about God. We become the opposite of the kind of person God would have us be.

God wants you to be happy with what you have, and not waste your time wanting things.

Challenge: Let's play an opposite game. Take this piece of candy and *give* it to someone.

Special Days

The following lessons are arranged to cover a school year, beginning in the fall. They are designated for the holidays as they occur to give you specific suggestions. Remember that it is also possible to use most of these lessons without reference to the specific holiday. Prayer, thankfulness, witness, and so forth, which are the themes of these lessons, are appropriate anytime.

19 *CH 8-98*

The First Day

Object: a child-sized bicycle (two wheels)

Lesson: The first day of school or of any new adventure can be frightening. Trust God to help you.

Outline

Introduce object: How many of you can ride a two-wheeler—a bicycle like this?

1. It can be scary to face the first day of school or of a new adventure.

2. Trust God to be with you and to help with the scary feeling.

3. *Conclusion:* With God by your side, you don't need to be scared.

How many of you can ride a two-wheeler—a bicycle like this? If you can't ride one now, I'm sure you have thought about it.

Do you remember the first time you got on one or thought about riding one? It is a scary feeling. You don't know what is going to happen to you. You don't know if you will be able to do it. But you do know that you want to ride one and that you need to get on to learn. It makes you feel both excited and afraid.

That's how we feel about the first day of school or of any big adventure. We are supposed to feel that way—scared, excited, nervous. Our stomach feels funny. We call that "butterflies" in our stomach—not because we really swallow butterflies but because it feels that way. Everybody feels this way sometimes. When you really do the new thing—when you find out it's not so bad—the funny feeling in your stomach goes away.

There is something that helps. You remind yourself that God takes care of you all of the time. He will not let something bad happen to you when you pray to him and trust him. He will go with you and he will help you. You are not alone. You can ask him to help you feel less scared. Ask him to help you like the first day of school or the big new adventure you are starting. You can learn to look forward to new things.

With God at your side, you don't need to be scared.

Challenge: Tie this string around your finger to remind you that God is with you all of the time.

20

Work Is Good

(Labor Day)

Object: work tools *(I used a shovel and a pen.)*

Lesson: Work is a God-given responsibility.

Outline

Introduce object: Labor Day is the day we celebrate work.

1. Gód gives us all work to do.
2. God makes us strong and smart enough to do it.
3. *Conclusion:* Thank God that you *can* work.

Labor Day is the day we celebrate work. There are many different kinds of work people do. The shovel I brought with me today is used by people who have to dig dirt in their jobs. They might have to dig ditches for pipelines, dig holes to plant trees, dig up tree stumps to plant fields, or dig foundations for buildings. It is hard work to dig up dirt. It hurts your back. You have to be strong to do it. More people work with this small pen. They have to write down words or numbers or designs. That's work too because you have to think hard.

Work is good. God wants us to do our work. Everybody

has work to do—even you! How many of you have t_
up your toys? How many of you go to nursery schoo_
kindergarten? How many of you help your mothers? W_
all have work.

We thank God that we *have* work to do! Work keeps us busy, helps us learn, and makes us feel like we are doing something good.

Think what the reasons would be for *not* working. If you were always sick, you could not work. If you could not move your arms and legs, you could not work. If you were not smart enough, you could not work. God made you smart and strong. Thank God you *can* work.

Challenge: This week do some work for God: help around the church, do something for the parents God gave you. [*The children could be assigned a specific job like pushing in the chairs, collecting papers, and so forth.*]

(World Communion)

Object: a cross

Lesson: The universality of believers

Outline

Introduce object: You have all seen this before. Can you tell me what it is?

1. People all over the world use the symbol of the cross just as they use the bread and wine [*juice*].

2. The Holy Catholic Church includes all of the people who love Jesus.

3. *Conclusion:* I like thinking that there are people all around this whole wide world who love my Jesus too.

You have all seen this before. Can you tell me what it is? Yes, it is a cross. Can you tell me what it means to us? Yes, it reminds us that Jesus died on a cross for us. People all over the world use the shape of the cross.

It is because Jesus died on a cross that we have communion or the Lord's Supper, which we are having today. Jesus wanted his followers to remember what he did. He said that the bread reminds us that his body was killed and hung on the cross. The red drink reminds us of the bleeding when he died. People all over the world use bread and different kinds of drink to help them remember how Jesus died. That is why this is World Communion Sunday.

Do you remember hearing the words "I believe in the Holy Catholic Church"? We say them in the Apostles' Creed. The words "Holy Catholic Church" mean the people who love Jesus. There are people who love Jesus all over the world. They speak different languages and may show this love in different ways than we do, but God loves them too! I like thinking that there are people all around this whole wide world that love my Jesus too.

Challenge: (Make crosses from sticks or paper or with crayons. Have the children retell the importance of the cross.)

22

People Power

(Mission Sunday)

Object: a manually operated toy *(I used a propeller on a stick, which is set in motion by placing the stick between the palms and rubbing quickly in one direction.)*

Lesson: God used people to spread his word.

Outline

Introduce object: Just sitting here, this twirler doesn't look like much to play with.

1. Just as the toy is people-powered, God uses people to bring his message. *(Explain what missionaries are.)*

2. You can be God's people power here and now.

3. *Conclusion:* This is a day to think about and pray for missionaries. It is also a day to think about being a missionary yourself.

Just sitting here, this twirler doesn't look like much to play with. It is doing nothing and does not look all that interesting. That is because this toy is people-powered *(run by a person)*. When you pick it up and rub it through your hands like this, it twirls around and takes off into the air. With people power it goes somewhere.

This is the special day we remember the missionaries. They are using their power to tell people about God's love around the world. Yes, God uses people power to tell all the people of the world about him. Special people called *missionaries* go to other countries and live with people who don't know about him. They love these people because of God and tell them about his great love for them. It is a wonderful thing to be a missionary.

Perhaps some of you will be God's people power and go to other countries when you grow up. You don't have to wait until then, though. Just as you don't have to be very old or very strong to work this toy with people power, you don't have to be very old or strong to be God's messenger right here at home. You can tell your friends about Jesus. You can bring people to Sunday school. You can look for ways to help older people. While you are doing these things, you can tell people that God loves them.

This is a day to think about and pray for missionaries. It is also a day to think about being a missionary yourself.

Challenge: (Give each child the name of a missionary to pray for.)

23
Much for Which to Be Thankful
(Thanksgiving)

Object: a picture of a refugee child

Lesson: You have so much for which to be thankful.

Outline

Introduce object: This is a picture of a child in a country where there is war.

1. A refugee child has no home, clothes, toys, and so forth.
2. Which of these things do you have?
3. *Conclusion:* You have *all that*? How much you have to be thankful for this Thanksgiving.

This is a picture of a child in a country where there is war. He has no home because it was burned down. He has only the clothes he can carry with him. His family has no furniture because it was lost with his house. He has no place to go because there is a war in his village and he can't go back there. Often he does not have enough to eat. He doesn't think about what foods he would like to have but whether he can get enough to keep him from being hungry. He is smiling because he is alive and so is the rest of his family. He has a lot for which to be thankful.

Would you like to be this child? Can you imagine what it would be like to have no home, few clothes, no toys, and poor food? How many of you have a home to live in? Is it a nice home? How many of you have a bed to sleep in and chairs to sit on? How many clothes do you have to wear? Do you have toys to play with? Do you have enough food to eat and a refrigerator to keep it in? You have *all that*? How much you have to be thankful for this Thanksgiving!

Challenge: Go home and try to count your toys. Look around your home. Then tell God all of the things for which you are thankful.

24

I Shall Not Want

(Thanksgiving)

Object: a filled lunchbox *(Psalm 23:1)*

Lesson: "I shall not want" means that God will take care of all of my needs.

Outline

Introduce object: I would like to talk about the first line of Psalm 23 [*hold lunchbox but keep it closed*].

1. When I eat the lunch, I will not *want* for food.

2. The Shepherd will give me what I need, so I will not have to *want* for it.

3. *Conclusion:* I am thankful this Thanksgiving that the Lord is my Shepherd.

I would like to talk about the first line of Psalm 23 *(hold lunchbox but keep it closed]*. I'm sure you have heard it before. It says, "The Lord is my shepherd, I shall not want."

When I was your age, I use to think that it was nice that the Lord is my Shepherd, but why wouldn't I *want* him? I was older before I learned what that really meant. Let me tell you so you will know now, even though you are young.

If I am hungry, I *want* food [*tone of voice is important*]. I am hungry now so I hope there is something in my lunchbox. Oh, good; it's full! After I eat this I will not *want* anymore. That is what Psalm 23:1 means. The Lord is my Shepherd—a shepherd is the person who gives the sheep what they need. In this case I am a sheep. I shall not *want* because my Shepherd will take care of everything I need.

Now that makes sense! I am thankful this Thanksgiving that the Lord is my Shepherd.

Challenge: Let's sing these words to the tune of "I have the Joy, Joy, Joy, Joy, Down in my Heart."

> Oh, the Lord is my shepherd, I shall not want.
> I shall not want, I shall not want.
> Oh, the Lord is my shepherd, I shall not want.
> I shall not want today.

25

A Shining Christmas Tree

(Advent)

Object: a ceramic Christmas tree *(house or church)* with a light on inside

Lesson: The spirit of love and joy at Christmas comes from within you and shines its glow on others.

Outline

Introduce object: Watch what this Christmas tree can do.

1. The light shines from the tree onto others as the spirit of Christmas shines from you onto others.

2. Advent is the time of year when we spread God's love and joy to others.

3. *Conclusion:* I love this time of year—don't you?

Watch what this Christmas tree can do. When I plug it in, the lights go on. Where does the light come from? There is a light bulb inside of the tree that shines through these small holes with colored beads in them. The light comes from within this tree and shines out for everyone to see and enjoy.

This is the way the Spirit of Christmas starts—with a

glow from inside of us. It shines out through you
the things you say and the things you do. Th
Christmas is the warm, loving, joyful feeling t
when we think of how Jesus was born as a bɛ
God loves us so much that he sent his only Son
us.

These weeks before Christmas are called *Advent*. Advent means we are getting ready for Christmas Eve. We
are beginning to celebrate. Advent is the time of year when
we spread God's love and joy to others. I love this time of
year; don't you?

Challenge: Do something to show this love: sing a song, give
a hug, do a good deed, give a special smile.

26

Look for the Good

(Advent)

Object: a magnifying glass

Lesson: Keep a positive attitude.

Outline

Introduce object: Have you ever looked through a magnifying glass?

1. Magnifying glasses make things look big.

2. In keeping with the Christmas spirit, look for *good* things to make big.

3. *Conclusion:* What would you rather have made big for real, something ugly or something lovely?

Have you ever looked through a magnifying glass? How does it make things look? That's right, they look bigger. You might use a magnifying glass to look at a grain of salt or an insect wing or a small leaf. I use one to read very small print. You can make thoughts and actions and events bigger without a magnifying glass by talking about them and thinking about them a great deal. Then they become big in your life.

With a magnifying glass you have a choice of what you want to make big. You do with your thoughts as well. Perhaps somebody says something unkind. You have a choice of whether to make a big deal out of it or to forget it. Perhaps a friend wouldn't share. You can carry on about it, like making it bigger with a magnifying glass, or you can say, "I don't care," and go on to something else. What do you think Jesus would want you to do?

This is the Advent season, the time of year we get ready to celebrate Jesus' birth. It's the time of year to think about the good things people do. It is a time of year to look for good things to make bigger. It is the time of year to spread love and peace on the earth, to practice kindness and goodwill to people.

What would you rather have made big for real, something ugly or something lovely?

Challenge: (Give each child a piece of paper with the shape of a magnifying glass.) Think of what you would like to make bigger and have someone write it inside of the magnifying glass on this paper. [*If the shape is large enough, the children could draw a picture of it.*]

27
Waiting
(Advent)

Object: a stopwatch or a watch with a second hand

Lesson: Patience

Outline

Introduce object: Do you know how long a minute it? This stopwatch will tell me exactly.

1. Waiting for something you want can be difficult.

2. God will give you patience if you ask for it.

3. *Conclusion:* Make yourself busy with doing good things, and Christmas will come—all in God's time!

Do you know how long a minute is? This stopwatch will tell me exactly. Hold your breath when I say go. I'll tell you when the minute is up. Are you ready? Go! No cheating. [*Wait—one minute!*] Okay, the minute is up. From the looks on your faces, I can tell that was a very long minute for you.

Sometimes time goes very fast—especially when you are busy. Other times it seems to take forever—especially when you are waiting for something you want. However, each minute is the same on the watch. It just doesn't seem this way.

God tells us to have patience when we must wait for things. We usually don't get what we want *when* we want it! Even adults have to learn to wait. Waiting can be hard but God will give us patience if we ask for it. If we don't have patience, we tend to get angry with ourselves or other people or rush ahead and settle for less than we could have. If we do have patience, we will wait for the time it takes.

The Advent season, the time of year we wait for Christmas, is a difficult time to have patience. Make yourself busy with doing good things and Christmas will come—all in God's time.

Challenge: When you get home, have someone time a minute when you are busy. Remember the minute here, and see which one is easier.

28

Christmas Giving

(Christmas)

Object: an empty gift box

Lesson: The best gift is an act of love.

Outline

Introduce object: Would you like to find out what is inside this gift box?

1. The best things can't be put in boxes.

2. The best birthday present for Jesus would be to do an act of kindness in his name.

3. *Conclusion:* What will *you* do?

Would you like to find out what is inside this gift box? I'll open it. Look, it's empty. No, that isn't a mistake, I want to tell you that the very best things to give cannot be put in a box.

What God gave *us* at Christmas was the baby Jesus. You couldn't put him in this box. God also gave us love, joy, and hope. The angels sang about peace on earth. You can't put peace and kind words in a box. The angels also sang about goodwill toward men. Goodwill means you feel good about people and want to help them and make their life happier. You can't put acts of kindness and thoughts of love in a box.

Let's all give a birthday present to the baby Jesus. What can we give? He would like us to do something nice for somebody. What can you do that will make somebody feel better?

The best birthday present for Jesus would be to do something kind because you love Jesus. What will *you* do?

Challenge: Tell me what you are going to do, and I will write it on a piece of paper and put it in the box.

29

A Newborn Baby

(Christmas)

Object: a newborn baby *(if you can't get one, use a realistic doll)*

Lesson: Jesus came to earth as a real baby.

Outline

Introduce object: This is little Daniel. He is only a few weeks old.

1. Jesus was born a real baby like this many years ago.
2. His birth was so important that we are still celebrating it.
3. *Conclusion:* I'm glad we remember the wonderful night Jesus was born.

This is little Daniel. He is only a few weeks old. I'm glad his parents let me bring him to be here with you because he will help us think about what Christmas is really all about. See how small and cute he is? There is something very special about a newborn baby!

That is why we celebrate Christmas. Jesus was born a tiny baby like this one. He was born a long time ago in Bethlehem. He probably cried for a little while and then went to sleep. Can you imagine God's only Son being a tiny baby like this so many years ago? I wish I could have been there to see the baby Jesus, but I can look at little Daniel and think of what it must have been like. We would be in a stable with the animals, and Mary and Joseph would be smiling.

Jesus was a special baby. He had a big job to do when he grew up. Imagine God's Son living on the earth! His birth was so important that we are still celebrating it. I'm glad we remember the wonderful night Jesus was born.

Challenge: Let's sing "Happy Birthday" to Jesus.

30

Silent Night

(Christmas)

Object: a lamp with a thick shade

Lesson: To clarify the meaning of "Round yon Virgin Mother and child"

Outline

Introduce object: I brought this lamp with me to help explain the Christmas song "Silent Night, Holy Night."

1. The light shines around the lamp.

2. Calmness and light from an inner glow shone around the mother and child.

3. *Conclusion:* It was a wonderful night.

I brought this lamp with me to help explain the Christmas song "Silent Night, Holy Night." Listen carefully to the words:

> Silent night! holy night!
> All is calm, all is bright,
> Round yon Virgin Mother and Child!
> Holy Infant, so tender and mild,
> Sleep in heavenly peace,
> Sleep in heavenly peace.

Most of the words are pretty clear but when I was young I wondered who *Round John Virgin was*!

Take a look at the lamp. When I turn this lamp on, the light shines around the lamp. If we use the language of the song, we could say, "The light shines round yon lamp."

The song says that all is calm, all is bright round yon Virgin Mother or around the virgin mother—that's Mary and child. The song is a lullaby. It tells them to sleep. It has been a long day, and Mary and Joseph are tired. New babies need sleep. For a while everything is calm. There is a warm, inner glow shining around the mother and child. They sleep in heavenly peace.

Of course, we know that soon the shepherds will be on their way. The angels will tell them about Jesus being born. But for now, let's let them sleep in heavenly peace. It was a wonderful night!

Challenge: When you go to sleep tonight, think of the new sleeping baby.

31

A New Start

(New Year)

Object: new shoes

Lesson: A new year means a new chance to go where God wants you to go.

Outline

Introduce object: I always enjoy getting new shoes, don't you?

1. Where will you walk with these new shoes?

2. What good places will you go and good things will you do with this new year?

3. *Conclusion:* What will *you* do?

I always enjoy getting new shoes, don't you? They make your feet feel like you want to jump and run and go new places. They look shiny and clean like a fresh start. We often think about the size and color of new shoes we get, but there is something else you can think about: "Where will I go in these new shoes?"

This is a new year. The old year is over, and we start again with January. God wants us to do this for a special reason. It gives us a time to think about what *new* things we can do with this new year and what *new* places we can go with this new year. We put the past behind us and think clean and new and ready to go.

Where will *I* go in these new shoes? I'll make sure I go to church in them often. I want to go to nursing homes and visit old people and try to cheer them up and keep them from feeling lonely. I'll wear the shoes while getting things that will help people. If you had a brand-new pair of shoes right now, where would you walk in them?

This is a New Year. It is a time for thinking about what new things you can do. As we celebrate this year, let's make promises about the new good things we can do and the new good places we can go, about being helpful and kind, about doing what our parents want us to do, about being the kind of person God wants us to be. You can do many things with this new year. What will you do?

Challenge: Pretend God has given you new, invisible shoes. You will wear them to do what he wants you to do and to go where he wants you to go.

32

You Are God's Light

(New Year)

Object: a flashlight

Lesson: witnessing

Outline

Introduce object: Have you ever been in a storm where the lights go out, and it is totally dark?

1. You need a flashlight to see in the dark.

2. You are God's flashlight to shine his love and show others the way.

3. *Conclusion:* A light is brightness, gentleness, and hope.

Have you ever been in a storm where the lights go out, and it is totally dark? Have you ever been outside at night when there has been no moon, especially where there were no streetlights? Have you ever gone into a room with no windows? When you are in the dark, a flashlight would be a very important thing to have.

Jesus said that you are the light of the world. That means that *you* are a flashlight. You can help other people see the way. You can tell them about Jesus because he is where they can find the light. God counts on you to do this.

This is a new year. We talk about the new year as a new start—a chance God gives us to do what he wants us to do—a new time to do what is right.

God has given you this new year—all of us—so that we will have a new time to remember and believe that we are his flashlights—each one of us. We must shine his love on other people and show them the way God wants us to go. A light is brightness, gentleness, and hope.

Challenge: Take a flashlight into a dark room or closet at home and remember that God wants you to shine as brightly as that light.

33

Stand Up for the Right

(Epiphany)

Object: a cooked and uncooked spaghetti noodle

Lesson: Stand up and act on what you believe.

Outline

Introduce object: Hold the noodles while you begin with a discussion of Epiphany.

1. A wet noodle doesn't know what to do.

2. A dry noodle can stand up; it can be used.

3. *Conclusion:* Can you be like the wise men and have the courage to follow Jesus?

We are still in the Christmas season because today we are going to talk about *Epiphany.* Epiphany is the special day we remember the wise men who came from the east to find the baby Jesus. The reason they have their own day is because it took them a long time to find Jesus. They were just *beginning* their trip when the shepherds came to the stable that wonderful night when Jesus was born.

The wise men had to know exactly what they believed and they had to act on it. They had to go a very long way, and it was not an easy trip. They couldn't be like this wet or cooked noodle that is droopy and funny looking. Try to stand it up and it falls right down again. This noodle isn't good for anything. In fact, it's cold, so I'll have to throw it away. People who are like this wet noodle can't make up their minds what they believe. They wouldn't be able to stand up and say: "You shouldn't bully little kids; it's not right." "You should not swear; God doesn't like it." "You should do what your mother tells you to do." "You should say nice things to people." "Cheer up—God loves you!"

This dry noodle is like the wise men who knew that they were looking for Jesus and they didn't care how hard it would be to find him. I can use this dry noodle to point out things. It doesn't get floppy. People like this are determined, and know and do what is right. They will seek Jesus—like the wise men. Can you be like the wise men and have the courage to follow Jesus?

Challenge: Feel the difference between these noodles. Which one would you like to be? Ask your mother for a noodle at home.

34

Two Long Years
(Epiphany)

Object: a child of about two years of age

Lesson: Be dedicated to your task.

Outline

Introduce object: This is Jamie. He is about two years old.

1. The wise men traveled for about two years under difficult circumstances.

2. A person dedicated to his/her task is willing to work hard for it.

3. *Conclusion:* How much work would you be willing to do or how far would you be willing to go for Jesus?

This is Jamie. He is about two years old. He is not a little baby anymore. He can walk and talk and gets into everything now. I have him with me to show you about how old Jesus was when the wise men finally found him.

The wise men saw a sign in the sky. They were excited because it meant that a king had been born to the Jews. They packed up their camels and set out to find him. It was dangerous to travel in those days. There were no good roads such as we have today to travel on or motels (with or without swimming pools) to sleep in at night. The wise men had to sleep alongside of the path most times and cook their own meals. Robbers would hide by the side of the road and steal from the people passing by, even beat them up. But for about *two* years they traveled on their dangerous and difficult trip—as long as it has taken Jamie to grow from a tiny baby to a little boy like this. They were willing to work very hard for what they know was right.

Sometimes we complain when our mothers want us to do a chore for them—such a small thing. Are you willing to do your chores? Are you willing to help your teachers clean up the room? Are you willing to work hard at your task? Are you willing to work as hard as the wise men?

How much would you be willing to do or how far would you be willing to go for Jesus?

Challenge: Draw a picture of one of the wise men.

35

A Good Example

(Presidents' Day)

Object: pictures or silhouettes of Washington and Lincoln.

Lesson: Characteristics of greatness include being God-fearing.

Outline

Introduce object: Do you know who these men are?

1. Washington and Lincoln are important men in the history of our country.

2. What made them great was their honesty, compassion, bravery, ability to work hard, and their fear of God.

3. *Conclusion:* Are these things you can do? Then perhaps some day you will be a great leader.

D o you know who these men are? They are very important in the story of our country. Both of them were presidents. Washington was the first president of our country. He also did much to help us to *have* a country of our own. This is Lincoln. Lincoln was a well-loved president. He was wise and kind. One important thing he did was to free the slaves.

This time of year we celebrate Presidents' Day. It is a good time to think about what makes these men great, why they were so important, why they did so many good things, and why we still remember them today.

These men were brave—they did what was right even when it was hard. They were kind to people—they would help people whenever they could. They worked hard for their country. These men also loved God and wanted to do his will. They prayed to God and asked God what they should do. We call this being *God-fearing*. Used in this way God-fearing doesn't mean to be afraid of God but to trust and want to follow God. We should really say *God-trusting*.

These are some of the things that made Washington and Lincoln great men. Are these things you can do? Then perhaps some day you will be a great leader.

Challenge: (Give the children a copy of the pictures to take home, display, and remember the characteristics of greatness.)

36

Pray

(World Day of Prayer)

Object: a telephone extension cord

Lesson: Prayer is having your own line to God.

Outline

Introduce object: This is a phone cord. It is used to make a telephone reach farther.

1. A phone cord makes a telephone reach many places.

2. Your prayer line to God reaches anywhere.

3. *Conclusion:* God is always ready to talk to you. What a wonderful God he is. Don't forget to pray to him!

This is a phone cord. It is used to make a telephone reach farther. With a cord this long, the phone at your house might reach all the way to your bedroom. Or it might be able to reach into your basement.

Prayer is like having your own line to God. The best part about it, though, is that it can reach anywhere you want to go. You don't have to worry about running out of cord or stumbling over it. Your line to God is invisible and as long as it needs to be, as long as you can imagine it to be. All you have to do is start praying and God is on the line. You never get a busy signal and you don't have to wait for God to get to the phone.

This is World Day of Prayer. People all over the world are remembering to make a special prayer—like a special phone call. Imagine, all these calls and the lines are still not all busy! God is always ready to talk to his people—to you. What a wonderful God he is. Don't forget to pray to him!

Challenge: Go home and see how long your phone cord is and remember how much longer your line to God is.

37

A Soft Heart

(Lent)

Object: two balloons—one filled with water, one filled with water and frozen

Lesson: Hard hearts are dangerous.

Outline

Introduce object: Lent is the word we use to talk about the time we get ready for Easter. [*Hold balloons to keep their attention while the word* Lent *is explained.*]

1. An angry or a jealous heart is cold, like the frozen balloon.

2. Lent is a time for a soft, kind heart like the other balloon.

3. *Conclusion:* In this season of Lent, make sure your heart is kind and helpful, like the heart of Jesus.

*L*ent is the word we use to talk about the time we get ready for Easter. It is like the time before Christmas that we call Advent. It is a time for thinking about the wonderful thing Jesus did when he died on the cross for us. It is a time to think about what is in our hearts and what kind of a person Jesus wants each of us to be.

How many of you have seen balloons filled with water like this red balloon? Sometimes we play games tossing them to each other and seeing who gets wet. This red balloon is filled with water and it sloshes. It is soft to carry and throw. This blue balloon was filled with water, but I put it in the freezer, and now it is filled with ice. It is cold and hard. It would be dangerous to throw this.

When you get angry or jealous or mean we say that you have a *hard heart*. Your heart can be soft and happy like this red balloon. If you let yourself become spoiled or selfish or unkind, then it is as if your heart is frozen and hard like this blue balloon. You wouldn't want that to happen!

In this season of Lent, make sure your heart is kind and helpful, like the heart of Jesus.

Challenge: (Give each child a balloon with water in it and have them place it in their freezer at home, so they can explain to their parents about a hard heart. Caution: Put less water in the balloons, and they will be less likely to break.)

38

Give Up Something for Lent

(Lent)

Object: something you like well enough to give up for Lent *(I used chocolate chip cookies).*

Lesson: Sacrificing to remember Jesus' sacrifice.

Outline

Introduce object: My very favorite thing to eat is a chocolate chip cookie.

1. Giving up something helps us remember that Jesus gave his life for us.

2. Giving up something we *like* helps us remember more often.

3. *Conclusion:* Each time I want to eat a cookie but do not eat one, I will remember to thank Jesus for what he did.

$\mathbf{M}$y very favorite thing to eat is a chocolate chip cookie. Yummy chocolate chips in a sweet, crisp cookie. My mouth waters just looking at this cookie. I can eat chocolate chip cookies every day, all day.

Because I like them so much, they can help me get ready

for Easter. When you choose something that you like very much to eat or to do, and then you decide you will not eat or do it until Easter comes, it is called "Giving up something for Lent." Lent is the forty days before Easter week. Giving something up helps us think about Jesus giving up his life for us. Giving up something we *like* helps us remember often, because we will think often about wanting to have it. Then we have a reason to remember often why we gave it up.

Each time I think about how I would like a chocolate chip cookie, I will think about Jesus' being willing to die for me. Each time I want to eat a cookie but do not eat one, I will remember to thank Jesus for what he did.

Challenge: (Ask each child what he/she would be willing to give up for Lent.)

39

Good Thoughts

(Lent)

Object: wild bird seed

Lesson: Think positive thoughts as a way to prepare to celebrate Easter.

Outline

Introduce object: I bought this wild bird seed for our pet parakeet.

1. A parakeet sorts out the seeds, taking what is good for him and leaving the rest.

2. People also should think good, positive thoughts— especially in preparation for Easter.

3. *Conclusion:* The best way to prepare, or get ready, is to think good thoughts and be thankful for the wonderful meaning of Easter.

I bought this wild bird seed for our pet parakeet. It has different kinds of seeds in it. What I didn't know was that our parakeet can't eat all of these seeds. She can only eat the little ones. We have a smart bird, though, because she picks out the seeds that are good for her and leaves the rest on the bottom of the cage.

People are supposed to do this too. There are many things we can talk and think about but not all of them are good for us. The Bible tells us to think about things that are good and kind and true. When we think about things that are bad and wrong, we become people that can only see that. If you think about doing well, being kind, and having good things happen, this is what you get! If you are looking for bad things, you can always find them. If you think you will not be able to do something, you probably won't.

This is the season of Lent—the time to prepare ourselves for Easter. The best way to prepare, or get ready, is to think good thoughts and be thankful for the wonderful meaning of Easter.

Challenge: (Have each child tell you something good.)

40

It's Your Choice

(Lent)

Object: a candle and a match

Lesson: God tells you through your conscience what is right. It is up to you to choose to do it.

Outline

Introduce object: Let me light this candle, and we will watch the flame burn.

1. Would you choose to put your hand in this flame?

2. Will you choose to follow your conscience and do what is right just as Jesus did?

3. *Conclusion:* He knew it was right and he chose to die.

Let me light this candle, and we will watch the flame burn. Should I put my hand into this flame? What do you think will happen if I do?

What if I gave you all your own candle to hold and left you alone with it? If there was no one watching you, what would you do with your candle? You would have a choice. You could listen to what your parents and teachers have told you, or you could choose to put your hand into the flame and see for yourself what would happen. Hopefully a small voice inside of you will tell you not to touch the flame because you will burn your hand. You might even then drop the candle and start a fire. The small voice that speaks inside of you is called your *conscience*. A good conscience is a great thing to have. It reminds you of what your parents have said and what God wants you to do. It tells you to make the right decision—to do the right thing. Will you choose to listen to your conscience?

This is the season of Lent. We are remembering that Jesus had a choice. He knew God wanted him to die for us, but he could have decided not to do it. He listened to God. He did what he had to do. He knew it was right and he chose to die.

Challenge: (Have the children tell of a situation where they made the right choice. For example, crossing the street, putting away toys, not hitting, sharing belongings, and so forth.)

41

Tools of Kindness

(Lent)

Object: a toolbox with common tools

Lesson: God has given us all the tools for making our world a better place. We need to use them.

Outline

Introduce object: I have a toolbox right here with screwdrivers, a wrench, a hammer and some nails, and a few other strange-looking things.

1. There are tools for fixing things around the house.

2. We have tools for helping people: a friendly smile, willing hands, kind words, and helpful acts.

3. *Conclusion:* In this season of Lent, we need to check our kindness toolbox and make sure everything we need is there. Do you have all of your tools?

I have a toolbox right here with screwdrivers, a wrench, a hammer and some nails, and a few other strange-looking things. The things are here that I need to keep the house running smoothly by fixing little things that break. I need all of these tools.

Just as there are tools for fixing things around the house, so are there tools for kindness. The tools of kindness are important in keeping things running smoothly around your house. They fix sad faces and hurt feelings. They make people happy and help them to be nice to each other. You have these things if you are willing to use them.

One of them is a friendly smile. Do you have a friendly smile? Another is a helping hand. Look at your hands. Can you use them to help other people? Still another is a cheerful voice. Can you say things like: "Good morning." "Have a nice day." "Take care." "I love you." "God loves you." "I'm sorry." Every *act* of kindness you do is also a tool for happiness.

In this season of Lent, we need to check our kindness toolbox and make sure everything we need is there. Do you have all of your tools?

Challenge: Go home and practice using your tools. [*Repeat what they are.*]

42

Palm Sunday Celebration

(Palm Sunday)

Object: party hats, plates, cups, napkins, and so forth. Palm branches would be nice if they are available.

Lesson: Palm Sunday was like a big party celebrating Jesus' arrival.

Outline

Introduce object: Look at these party hats, paper plates, napkins, and cups. What do you think they are for?

1. Just as we celebrate today with party paper goods, the people in Jesus' day waved palm branches.

2. The people were welcoming a king but Jesus was more than that. He had come to die for their sins.

3. *Conclusion:* It was so important that we still celebrate it today!

Look at these party hats, paper plates, napkins, and cups. What do you think they are for? Yes, they are for a party. We are having one at our house for some friends who are coming to visit. When they see these special things ready for them, they will know how happy we are to see them.

The people in Jesus' day didn't have paper hats and plates and napkins. But they did have a special way of welcoming Jesus. They waved branches from palm trees. They didn't do that for just anybody. They were all excited because they thought Jesus was going to Jerusalem to be their king.

Jesus wasn't riding on a fancy horse or a big camel when he came (you know it was too long ago for a big car). Instead of riding into Jerusalem like he was really somebody, Jesus wanted to ride on a little donkey. This was supposed to tell the people that he was not there to be a fancy king. He had something more important to do—he was going to die for their sins.

The people didn't understand about Jesus' dying but they were right about one thing—Jesus coming to Jerusalem on that day was very important. It was so important that we still celebrate it today!

Challenge: (Give each child a party plate to wave and form a parade or cheering section. If possible use palm branches; they would be even more effective.)

43

The Lord's Supper

(Maundy Thursday)

Object: the elements of the Lord's Supper

Lesson: Jesus taught us to eat the bread and drink the wine to remember him.

Outline

Introduce object: The very best object lesson ever given was and still is called the Lord's Supper [*hold elements*].

1. Jesus taught the lesson, using the bread and drink on the table in front of him.

2. We still do the same today to remember what he did for us.

3. *Conclusion:* We do it because we love him and we want to remember him.

The very best object lesson ever given was and still is called the Lord's Supper. It was given by Jesus to his disciples. They were sitting around the table, eating. Jesus knew he was going to die for the sins of all the people he loved, and so he looked around at the disciples and taught them this lesson.

He picked up a piece of bread from the table and broke some off, telling the disciples to eat a piece of bread and remember his body, *broken for them*. Then Jesus picked up the cup with his drink, held it out, and told the disciples that they should take a drink and remember that Jesus gave his life for us. I'm sure the disciples were all listening very carefully to the things that Jesus was saying.

The bread and perhaps the drink that we use for the Lord's Supper, or (Communion, which we also call it) might be different from the kind Jesus used, but that doesn't matter. Jesus used what was on *his* table, and we should do the same. The lesson Jesus taught was how to remember him and what he did for us. We still do this today. We do it because we love him and we *want* to remember him.

Challenge: (Let the children have the bread and drink and express what they are doing and why.)

44

Suffered Under Pontius Pilate
(Good Friday)

Object: picture of a Roman ruler of that period.

Lesson: Jesus chose to die for us.

Outline

Introduce object: When we say the Apostles' Creed in church, we say the words, "suffered under Pontius Pilate, was crucified, dead, and buried." When we talk about Pontius Pilate we mean the man who was the judge of Jesus.

1. Pontius Pilate was the ruler at the time Jesus died. He didn't stand up for what he knew was right.

2. Jesus knew he should die and he chose to do it for you.

3. *Conclusion:* Each time you choose the right, you choose for Jesus.

When we say the Apostles' Creed in church we say the words "suffered under Pontius Pilate, was crucified, dead, and buried." When we talk about Pontius Pilate we mean the man who was the judge of Jesus (he is not the pilot of an airplane—they did not have airplanes then). Pilate was the Roman ruler at the time who decided whether people should die for their crimes.

What kind of a judge was he? Well, he decided after talking to Jesus that Jesus should be punished and then let go. When he told the people this, the people screamed, "No, no! You have to crucify [kill] him!" Pontius Pilate should have stuck by his decision to let Jesus go, but he went along with the crowd. He said Jesus could be crucified, that is, nailed to a cross. He knew Jesus had not done anything wrong but he went along with what other people wanted.

You will have many chances in your life to choose what is right or to go along with the people around you. If any or even *all* of these people are doing something that you know is wrong, you must choose to do the right thing. Each time you choose the right, you choose for Jesus.

Challenge: (Present a tray of "choices" including such things as matches, cigarettes, money to steal, and so forth. Have the children discuss their choices.)

Roman centurion.

45

Low in the Grave He Lay

(Easter)

Object: picture of a grave at that time.

Lesson: Jesus died, was buried, and rose again.

Outline

Introduce object: After Jesus died, he was taken down from the cross and placed in a grave. The grave looked like this.

1. The grave was low in the ground—and so we sing "Low in the grave he lay."

2. Jesus rose and is alive.

3. *Conclusion:* It is because he lives that we celebrate Easter.

After Jesus died he was taken down from the cross and placed in a grave. The grave looked like this [*show illustration*]. It had a big stone in front of it to protect the grave from robbers, because people at that time often put their nice things in the grave with the bodies. There are steps that go down, so that the little room which is cut from the stone is under the ground level where it is cooler.

When we sing the song, "Low in the grave he lay, Jesus, my Savior," we mean that he was placed in this low grave (it has nothing to do with the gravy we put on mashed potatoes). When Jesus died, he was carried down the steps and placed in the low grave the way people did at that time. We still bury people under the ground level today.

This big stone was then rolled in front of the grave. It was very heavy, and it took many men to move it. It set in a little groove to make it even harder to move away from the opening. Then soldiers were placed outside to make extra-sure that the disciples wouldn't come during the night and take the body away.

When all of this was done to keep the body in the grave, imagine the surprise of the soldiers when they found that the stone had been rolled away and Jesus was gone! They weren't just surprised; they were terrified. They were so scared that they ran away.

We sing the words "Up from the grave he arose" because our Jesus didn't stay dead. He became alive and rose up from the grave. It is because he lives that we celebrate Easter.

Challenge: (Sing the song with the children. Have them go home and sing it to their parents.)

46

Candy Eggs

(Easter)

Object: Easter eggs, real and candy.

Lesson: Eggs are a symbol of the new life.

Outline

Introduce object: Do you know why we eat candy eggs and real eggs at Easter?

1. From the eggs come new chicks ready for life.

2. From Easter comes our new life in Jesus.

3. *Conclusion:* When you eat candy eggs and real eggs at Easter, remember how they tell you that Easter is a time of new life, of a new beginning, of new excitement, a promise of a wonderful new life with Jesus.

Do you know why we eat candy eggs and real eggs at Easter? It is because eggs are a symbol of, or they stand for, what Easter means—just like the Christmas tree is a symbol of Christmas.

Think about real eggs! From them come wonderful little baby chicks—all fuzzy and cute—ready to begin a new life.

Beginning life, beginning a new life, that is what the egg is all about.

That is also what Easter is all about. Jesus rose from the grave and began a new life. Because of this we have a new life also—a new wonderful clean and free life in Jesus.

We eat the candy eggs because we often have candy at a party. On Easter we are celebrating. We are having a party because we are so happy that Jesus is alive. It is a day to sing and talk about how excited we are.

When you eat candy eggs and real eggs at Easter, remember how they tell you that Easter is a time of new life, of a new beginning, of new excitement, a promise of a wonderful new life with Jesus.

Challenge: (Give each child an egg and ask if he/she can tell why we eat eggs at Easter.)

47

A Gift

(Ascension Day)

Object: a small gift for the children such as a pencil, crayons, eraser, and so forth.

Lesson: When Jesus ascended into heaven, he promised that God would send the Comforter.

Outline

Introduce object: I have a gift for each of you today.

1. I have a gift for you so you will remember a still better gift given on Ascension Day.

2. When Jesus went back into heaven, he promised the people a Comforter.

3. *Conclusion:* Take this gift from me and remember the special gift promised on Ascension Day.

I have a gift for each of you today. It is this bright yellow pencil with a smile and the words "God loves you" [*or other small gift*]. I am giving you this gift today because I want to talk about a gift God gives his people. It is a very special gift—much better than a [pencil]. Listen carefully while I tell you about it.

After Jesus rose from the grave, he stayed with the apostles for a little while. Then it was time for him to go back to his Father in heaven. Before he left, on a day we remember and call Ascension Day, he said that God had a gift for the people. He called this gift "the Comforter" because when someone is sad, you comfort them. The people were sad about Jesus' leaving so they were to receive a comforter. This special gift would be the Holy Spirit, who would bring more love, help, peace, joy, and excitement than they could ever think of having.

We remember Ascension Day today because Jesus, when he left the earth, promised us a special gift. We can't see Jesus walking around anymore as the people could back then, but we can still feel he is with us—and we have his special gift.

Take this gift from me and remember the special gift promised on Ascension Day.

Challenge: Go home and tell your parents why you have this gift today.

48

A Mighty Rushing Wind

(Pentecost)

Object: a strong fan

Lesson: The Holy Spirit came with the sound of a mighty rushing wind, the strong but gentle Comforter.

Outline

Introduce object: This fan makes a pretty strong wind.

1. The Comforter came with the sound of a mighty rushing wind and a flame that didn't burn anything.

2. The Holy Spirit or Holy Ghost is someone special who is still here to help today.

3. *Conclusion:* He gives love, peace, joy, patience, and happiness. Just ask him.

This fan makes a pretty strong wind. Look at how it can blow things around. Do you remember that when Jesus went away he promised the people a Comforter? The apostles were all together in a house, and they heard a sound of a strong, or mighty, rushing wind. It must have sounded like a terrible storm. Then little flames like fire appeared and sat on the apostles. The strong wind—much stronger than the wind from this fan—didn't blow the house apart. It didn't even blow out the flames. The flames didn't burn anything. The wind and the flames were signs to show the apostles that the Comforter had come, and that he was really something special.

The apostles began to feel wonderful and excited. They started speaking in different languages. They began to know things that they did not know before. The Holy Spirit, or the Holy Ghost, as we sometimes call him, had come—the powerful but gentle Comforter—the strong force sent by God for his people. That is why we say in church the words "Father, Son, and Holy Ghost." God had kept his promise.

The Holy Spirit or Holy Ghost is still here today. Are you sad and need comfort? He will comfort you. Do you need strength to do something hard? He will give you strength. He gives love, peace, joy, patience, and happiness. Just ask him.

Challenge: (Give the children a paper flame that doesn't burn or make a paper fan by folding a piece of paper accordion style. Have them retell what they remember.)

49

The Powerful Holy Spirit

(Pentecost)

Object: a thin latex glove which can be inflated

Lesson: The Holy Spirit is among us and is powerful.

Outline

Introduce object: Have you ever seen a glove like this?

1. Air has the power to blow up this glove and change it.

2. The Holy Spirit has the power in our lives to bring joy and help us do good.

3. *Conclusion:* If a little air can change this glove, think how the power of the Holy Spirit can change your life!

Have you ever seen a glove like this? It is used to protect your hands from harsh soaps or other things that might cause a rash on your hands. Doctors use them to make sure they do not spread germs. I can do something interesting with one. If I blow air hard enough into one, I can blow it up. Now, how many of you have ever seen a glove like this?

What did I say is inside of this glove? Yes, air. Air can do strange things. You can't see it but you can feel the air pushing the glove back out when I pinch it.

Today we are celebrating, or remembering in a special way, the coming of the Holy Spirit on the day called Pentecost. Pentecost is the day the gift that God promised came—the Comforter to stay with the people and help them. Now, you can't see the Holy Spirit but you can feel that he is there. You can feel his power even *more* than you can feel the invisible power in this glove. You can feel the joy he brings when we pray. You can feel the power he gives us to do good things when we ask for it. He makes us happy and excited and able to do anything God wants us to do. If a little air can change this glove, think how the power of the Holy Spirit can change your life!

Challenge: (Pass the glove around for the children to feel the air pass through the inside. Have them tell their parents about the Holy Spirit.)

50

Remember Your Mother

(Mother's Day)

Object: photographs of you and your mother

Lesson: Mother's Day is a special time to remember and thank our mothers.

Outline

Introduce object: I have some very old pictures to show you.

1. These pictures remind me of what my mother did for me.

2. Mother's Day is a special day to remember and thank your mother for what she does for you.

3. *Conclusion:* My mother is no longer living, so I cannot give her a hug and talk to her about all of the nice things she did for me. Make sure you give your mother a big hug today.

I have some very old pictures to show you. This picture was taken of my mother and me in our backyard. Here we are at the park. My mother was always taking care of me, teaching me things, and going places with me.

Today is Mother's Day. Mother's Day is the one very special day out of the whole year when we remember the mother God gave us. We should really remember our mothers more than that, but since we only have this one national day, we had better make it a good one!

Stop and think of all the things your mother does for you. She buys you clothes and makes sure they are kept clean. She makes good food for you to eat—even makes your favorite things. She teaches you how to clean your room and brush your teeth. She puts Band-Aids on your scrapes and gives you hugs when you hurt or feel sad. A mother is a wonderful, loving, caring person! Yes, we really need more than one day to remember her.

My mother is no longer living, so I cannot give her a hug and talk to her about all of the nice things she did for me. Be sure to give your mother a big hug today.

Challenge: Give your mother a big, big hug and thank her for *all* of the things she does for you. Thank God for your mother.

51

The Two of You Are a Team

(Father's Day)

Object: a mixer with detachable beaters, a bowl of batter

Lesson: Cooperate with your father to accomplish the job God has given him. Remember to thank him on his special day.

Outline

Introduce object: My mixer has two beaters that come out when I push this button.

1. One beater works slowly. Two working together get the job done.

2. Cooperate with your father—work as a team.

3. *Conclusion:* Remember to thank him and give him a big hug on his special day.

My mixer has two beaters that come out when I push this button. If I take one of these beaters out and leave the other one in, the mixer will not work well. It will mix a little but it would take forever to get the job done this way. With both of the beaters in place and working together, my batter is mixed fast.

Let's pretend one of these beaters is you and the other one is your father. If you work one at a time, it will take a long time to get the job done. If you work together, you will be a team and things will get done quickly.

Today is Father's Day. It is a day to think about your father and all of the things he does for you, and all of the things you do together. The two of you as a team can learn and work together. Go along with what your father says or wants. That is called *cooperating*. Cooperate when your father wants you to do something. He always tries to do what is best for you both. Just like the mixer, if you help him and he helps you, you will get the job done and have a neat time together.

Your father has a big job to do in raising you to be the kind of person God wants you to be. He does a lot of praying and worrying about you. Remember to thank him and give him a big hug on his special day.

Challenge: Tell your dad that you are a team. If you don't have a father, tell your grandpa!

52

Remember and Go Forth

(Closing Exercise)

Object: a memory box with objects from former lessons

Lesson: Remember what you have learned, and practice it until we meet again.

Outline

Introduce object: This is a memory box. In it are some of the objects I have used for lessons this year.

1. Do you remember the lessons these objects represent?

2. The most important things to remember are that God loves you and he wants you to love him back and to help other people.

3. *Conclusion:* Remember what you have learned, keep alive the feeling of love and kindness, practice what you know is right until we are back together again.

This is a memory box. In it are some of the objects I have used for lessons this year. Do you remember the new shoes we talked about that would go new places and do new things for God? Well, you can tell by looking at the shoes that they *have* traveled! Here is some of the wild bird seed that reminded us to sort out the good and bad things to think about and then to spend our time thinking about good, positive things. This glove was blown up to help us talk about the invisible power of the Holy Spirit. Here are some tools. Do you remember the tools of kindness?

When we come to the close of a program it is a good time to remember what we have learned. The most important things to remember are that God loves you, and he wants you to love him and follow him. Loving his Son, Jesus, using the power of the Holy Spirit, and trying to help other people are the ways to be happy.

Remember what you have learned, keep alive the feeling of love and kindness. Practice what you know is right until we are back together again.

Challenge: Keep a memory box of your own so we can talk about your memories when you come back.